# Take Part Books

# Guidelines

## including

## Take Part Starters

# Ward Lock Educational

First published by Penguin Education 1974
Revised edition published by Ward Lock Educational 1975
Second edition 1978

Reprinted 1981, 1982

Printed by David Green Printers Ltd, Kettering
for Ward Lock Educational
47 Marylebone Lane, London W1M 6AX
A Ling Kee Company
Made in Great Britain

Ward Lock Educational would very much like to thank David
and Christina Milman, both London primary school teachers,
for their invaluable help in producing the section 'Take Part
Topics' and for their assistance throughout.

# Contents Page

# Introduction

What *Take Part Books* are and why they are important

*Take Part Books* are dramatized adaptations of well-known and highly regarded children's stories. The adaptations have not simplified or diluted the stories, but retain the essential essence of the original message relayed direct to the child. One element, the dialogue, is lifted from the original almost without interference and, because there is little alteration, the material remains a valuable literary whole.

*Take Part Books* are designed to be read aloud by groups of children. Ideally the number of children in a group should equal the number of parts in the book being read, so that each child can choose, or be allotted, one part.

*Take Part Books* are unique in their use of mixed reading age levels within the text. Take Part is so structured that children who are at different levels within a reading age range of 6+ to 9+ can all read together regardless of their chronological age. This can provide an all-important context-support where parts with lower reading ages are surrounded and supported by more demanding ones. Hence children with less reading ability are gradually introduced to difficult words and phrases by carefully chosen 'key' words and also by a previous speaker who is a more able reader paving the ground. For an example of this, see the sample page on page 9. Slowly and imperceptibly this support is withdrawn as the story progresses and confidence is gained. Those children taking parts at the highest levels can be encouraged to reach out for the unabridged versions.

*Take Part Books* are particularly useful with small groups of readers each taking a part with a higher or lower reading age. Take Part makes reading a shared experience because it is a group activity which in turn helps to break down social and academic barriers. Not only is working together as a team a worthwhile experience in itself but such group participation greatly assists individuals with their reading problems and with their confidence. With Take Part, the group moves forward at its own pace with everyone participating fully on an equitable basis though at different levels. Take Part initiates an active response to reading since children are taking part themselves. In this way a Take Part session has more in common with a film or TV play than a passive sitting and reading.

*Take Part Books* are greatly enhanced when used in conjunction with tape or cassette recorders. Working towards a recording either of a whole book or just one chapter can, at its simplest, be a rewarding climax. At another level, children are encouraged to add their own sound effects. Places where these are appropriate are indicated by asterisks throughout the text. Besides enlarging their enjoyment and interest, such a device helps children interpret print in a 'sounding way' and is, of course, accessible to everyone. Of great importance is the sense of achievement children can get from such a recording and its play back, which leads to more self-involvement and a more critical approach to the fluency, characterization and 'telling' of the story in hand.

*Take Part Books* are flexible. They are useful adjuncts to other reading schemes currently in use in our schools. Moreover, in the section of this *Guidelines* entitled Take Part Topics, we hope to suggest ways of using them as bases for extended work beyond that of reading.

*Take Part Books* were devised and originated by Sheila Lane and Marion Kemp, both experienced London teachers and well-known writers of books on children's literacy. They have used Take Part with remarkable success in many primary schools.

## Take Part Starter Books

The books in this series, also devised by Sheila Lane and Marion Kemp, are intended to introduce children to the *Take Part* series. For full details, see page 61 of these *Guidelines*.

# Tips for teachers

Hints on classroom use

The following are a few suggestions on how Take Part might be
best used in the classroom. These tips have been culled from
the experience of teachers who have used Take Part to great
advantage.

## The importance of introductions

A great difference is made to the subsequent success of Take
Part if every story that is tackled is introduced to the children.
Without giving away the plot, background details can be
'brought alive', and characters and situations can be explored.
Initial enthusiasm and interest can be considerably enhanced
by such a run-through. If you refer to the section on suggestions
for further work, you will find many useful 'talking points'
which will help enliven introductions. This section may also
assist in providing ideas on reinforcing materials and resources
such as other books, pictures, posters and records which would
be useful to have available during an introductory session.

## Choosing characters

If children are coming to Take Part for the first time, and
especially if they are in unstreamed classes or open-plan
situations, it is probably better if the teacher allocates parts to
children at the appropriate reading level. One teacher found it
useful to allocate parts on the basis of fluency rather than just
reading ages alone. It is a good idea to ensure that there is
always a strong reader in the group who can give support. As
Take Part continues, teachers should ensure that there is a
systematic moving up to higher levels and that the more mature
readers are encouraged to tackle the unabridged stories.
Practice, familiarity and confidence with Take Part gradually
removes the necessity of teachers allocating parts. Children are
quite happy to do this themselves, especially since natural
leaders often emerge in their own organization of a Take Part
session. Further, letting children do it for themselves greatly
enlarges the vital social experience of Take Part.

## The role of the teacher once Take Part is under way

While teachers and children are still new to Take Part,
experience seems to suggest that it is better if the teacher
remains quite involved with initial readings, maybe taking on a
difficult part. Children seem to enjoy a teacher's stronger

characterization and having the teacher 'join in'. At the starting-off stage speed and fluency tend to hang together better. As Take Part begins to flourish and children gain confidence, teachers can withdraw almost entirely. It is a good idea if, from time to time, the teacher returns to 'breathe fresh life' into a story or assist with individual problems. In any case, Take Part tends to free teachers so that they can turn their attention in other directions.

## When and how often?

Obviously this can vary a great deal; teachers always adapt a technique to their own particular circumstances. One teacher who used Take Part frequently managed to read, and tape, three stories in six 20–30 minute sessions. Others have found Take Part useful when the children have come to the end of some other work, but still have time to fill in. Another teacher found *The Wind in the Willows* lasting nearly half a term on the basis of a couple of sessions a week involving an initial reading, further run-throughs, recording and follow-up activities.

## Tape recorders and sound effects

As we have already said in the Introduction, recording can be immensely valuable in Take Part sessions. In fact, many shy and inarticulate children have been able to take the first trembling step towards real reading by making the hoot of an owl or the sound of footsteps and afterwards hearing these played back. Confidence is established and a start, however small, is made so that the child feels a real sense of involvement and achievement. As children become used to sound communication, so this aids their fluency.

Once a well-produced recording has been made, it can be listened to whilst the text is followed from the book, or it can be used as a 'radio play' for other children to listen to. Sound effects can be produced from an enormous variety of objects found in the classroom alone. Indeed, discovering and listing such effects can be a useful activity in itself, besides amassing a repertoire to be made available for a Take Part recording. Here are a few suggestions of our own:

(a) a paper bag, blown up and popped, can reproduce the sound of Sir Basil's gun in *Parsley and the Herbs,*
(b) a metal waste-paper bin and a ruler can reproduce a variety of car noises for Commander Pott's Chitty-Chitty-Bang-Bang,
(c) pencils tapped on desks for building,
(d) books dropped on desks for the house falling down,
(e) wooden cotton reels banged on desks for banging noises,

(f) scissors squeaking shut for windows closing,
(g) water being poured into a waste-paper bin for floods.

## Take Part and drama

*Take Part Books* were never intended to provide scripted drama for primary school children. But they do offer stimulating starting off points for free and unscripted drama. Once familiarity with a story and its characters has been established, children could then expand and extend, through their own imagination and initiative, Take Part stories. There are many suggestions for improvised drama in the next section, Take Part Topics.

*Take Part Books* and unabridged versions of the same stories

Take Part is really a device to help children who have made a start to become more mature readers. It should involve the child – good stories invariably do this for children, it should get them reading almost as a by-product – their interest in the stories and 'taking part' will predominate, and it should be fun. It is, therefore, essential that, when the child feels ready and wants to, the unabridged versions of the Take Part stories are available on request. This is precisely what Take Part is all about: a stepping stone to real reading where the child sees reading as an activity that is worthwhile and enjoyable.

# Sample pages

## What Take Part looks like

**Chief**   And so he is not yours. If he outmatched you, he has bought his freedom.

**Magua**   The Indian prisoner is a spy.

**Chief**   Let him come forward. * Who are you?

**Uncas**   I am a Delaware.

**Magua**   The prisoner has changed his paint.

**Uncas**   Do not listen to the singing bird, O Great and Wise Chief.

**Magua**   Yesterday this man said he was a Huron.
Today he says he is a Delaware.
Tomorrow he will be a ...

**Hawkeye**   Mohican! Uncas! Show who you really are before the long knives reach you. Tear off your shirt and show the tattoo marks on your skin.

**Uncas**   Look! Will you harm a son of your father's fathers?

**Chief**   The sign of The Great Tortoise!

**Duncan**   This Mohican is the last of his great tribe.

Sample page from *The Last of the Mohicans*. Notice how Uncas and Magua are given context support by Hawkeye and the Chief.

**Tip**   I shout loud enough, don't I?

**Jack**   Yes, but the Saw-Horse has no ears.
Why don't you make him some?
Then you can tell him what to do.

**Tip**   That's a splendid idea. Watch me. * Now, I musn't make them too long or he'll look like a donkey. *

**Jack**   How is that?

**Tip**   Because a horse has bigger ears than a man, and a donkey has bigger ears than a horse.

**Jack**   If my ears were bigger, would I be a horse?

**Tip**   No friend, you'll never be anything but a Pumpkinhead, no matter how big your ears are. Now hold the horse while I make two holes in his ears. * There! CAN YOU HEAR ME SAW-HORSE? Whoa! Whoa! *

**Jack**   Come back! Come back!
Why don't you come back, Saw-Horse?

**Saw-Horse**   Here I am!

**Tip**   Whoops! * Now you've fallen over. You're a nice sort of horse, I must say. Why didn't you stop when I yelled,'Whoa?'

**Saw-Horse**   Does 'Whoa' mean to stop?

**Jack**   He's like me.
He doesn't know much.

**Saw-Horse**   What am I doing here anyway?

This sample page from *The Land of Oz* shows how voices can be used to produce a variety of dramatic sound effects. For reading age levels, turn to page 62.

# Take Part Topics

Suggestions for supportive and extended work

In this section we are saying something about each Take Part story, followed by a variety of suggestions for work which might surround or extend beyond these stories. Our suggestions are by no means comprehensive; they are simply starting points which teachers may find of interest, either for introducing and supporting Take Part itself or for using a Take Part story as the basis for further topic-orientated work.

# Beaverbird
*Ruth Underhill*

Most children are familiar enough with Red Indians from mass media to feel at home with Ruth Underhill's book, which is a real attempt to evoke the true world of the Indian, his customs and his ways of thought. This story of life among American Indians is ideally suited to an investigation of their culture.

## Topic: American Indians

A historical and geographical study of tribes could include homes – transport, hunting, tracking and fishing – weapons and war – superstitions – regional characteristics and customs.

Homes: the effect on designs of a nomadic existence (e.g. wigwams), the use of natural resources such as buffalo skins for building materials, the camp.

Transport: the central importance of the horse, its use in warfare and hunting by plains tribes, the horse-drawn litter and the canoe.

Hunting: the image of the brave as a hunter, the importance of game and the buffalo for meat and by-products, tracking and animal signs.

Weapons: bows and arrows, tomahawks, knives, clubs and latterly the rifle.

Superstitions: Indian gods, the idea of animal spirits, the importance of the medicine man and the totem pole.

Tribes: the characteristics of different tribes and how these might have been affected by the regions in which they lived. Tribal and individual names make an interesting study, as do tribal costume and forms of decoration.

## Language

A discussion of Indian names may well be fruitful. Many of these are based on the attributes of the person who holds them, e.g. Proudfoot, or on animal names, as with Beaverbird. Children could research the meanings of their own names and invent names for their friends based on their characteristics. A class list of invented names could be drawn up and poems and stories written using these names.

The idea of hunting could serve as a stimulus, the child being asked to imagine he was a hunting brave who had found a mysterious animal track and followed it. The theme of good and bad luck could provoke discussion on the children's own experiences and superstitious beliefs. The rhythms of percussion and the hunting song could lead to poetry writing. Themes such as the Song of the Hunter or the tribe praying for rain would lend themselves to this sort of treatment. The suggestion at the end of the book might be followed up with children writing a story or playscript telling of Mumu's wild life in the forest or of the lives of Red Fish and Beaverbird after they became brothers.

## Drama

Improvised drama and dance could be based on the tribal meeting or feast, centring round the totem pole and using percussion, with masks and poems written by the children. The meeting might be before a hunt or a part of a rainmaking ceremony. Similarly a day in the life of an Indian village could be explored through improvisation.

## Music

Percussion work follows naturally from the sounds that the Shellnose and Water People make on pages 20 and 21 of the book. Work might be based on signalling rhythms and the echo of repeated message and reply. Percussion instruments could be made, e.g. with yoghurt cartons or tins filled with dried peas, and then decorated. The sound qualities of the instruments could be emphasized by concentrating on dry, wooden sounds associated with the Shellnose tribe and liquid sibilants connected with the Water People.

## Mathematics

Discussion of Indian names for the months of the year could lead to comparative work on the derivation of our calendar names. Similar research could be done on the days of the week. The seasons can also be considered. This would lead to general mathematical work on time.

Map work might be used as an introduction to simple grid reference. Children could be given squared paper and asked to draw key points from the story into designated squares. These might include the forest, river, Water People's village, the secret place of Red Fish, the bear's cave etc.

## Art

Children could make paper or card masks. A large totem pole could be made from boxes piled on top of one another with noses and raffia or wool hair added. Scenes from Indian life might be painted on the back and sides. As a class activity, a frieze could be made showing incidents in Beaverbird's life, different groups being responsible for different aspects of the story.

Traditional Indian motifs could be used in pattern work, lino cuts and printing. Discussion of Indian decorative art could lead to needlework on pieces of Binca using patterns based on traditional motifs. Collages using felt and materials collected by the children could be made on hessian or card. These could be illustrations of Indian stories.

# Further Reading

## Non-fiction

**Cowboys** (Blackwell: Little Learning Library)

**Explorer 7: The Discovery of America** (Puffin)
*J. R. L. Anderson*
Here is outlined the whole fascinating story from prehistoric man, and his wanderings from Asia into Northern America across the Bering Strait when it was still land, to Columbus and the adventurers and settlers who followed in his wake.

**Explorer 8: The Day of the Cowboy** (Puffin)
*Kenneth Ulyatt*
A revealing look at what the cowboy's life was really like. Kenneth Ulyatt traces the history of the cowboy from the time the Conquistadors brought the first cattle to the Americas until the end of the last century, when barbed wire enclosed the free range, and the power of the old cattle kingdoms waned.

**Indians** (Blackwell: Little Learning Library)

**North American Indians** (Macdonald: Starters Long Ago)

**The Indians** (Ladybird)

**The Wagon Trail** (Macdonald: Starters Long Ago)

## Fiction

**Antelope Singer** (Puffin)
*Ruth Underhill*
A family of settlers on their way to California are abandoned by the wagon train and forced to spend a winter among the Indians.

**Beaverbird** (Puffin) *Ruth Underhill*

**Island of the Blue Dolphins** (Puffin)
*Scott O'Dell*
True story of an Indian girl marooned on a desolate island. Recently made into a film.

### Master Entrick (Puffin)
*Michael Mott*

One cold night in 1754 on his way home from school young Robert Entrick is kidnapped and taken as a slave to America. His new master is then murdered by Indians, so Robert is on his own with a stolen canoe and no chart! An exciting adventure for readers of 10 and over.

### North Against the Sioux (Puffin)
*Kenneth Ulyatt*

As he guided Colonel Carrington's secret expedition into the town, Portugee Phillips could see the Indian tepees pitched beside Laramie Creek from afar off. He was there to hear Red Cloud, the great chief, threaten war to all white men who ventured into Sioux territory. But still he went . . . .

### Pilgrims of the Wild (Puffin)
*Grey Owl*

Fifty years ago, Grey Owl was a trapper and guide in the Canadian backwoods, until one day he adopted two kitten beavers and started preserving life instead of destroying it.

### When the Legends Die (Puffin)
*Hal Borland*

# Brer Rabbit

*Joel Chandler Harris*

The story of the tricks that Brer Rabbit plays on his friends and their attempts at revenge is one that appeals to many children.

## Topic: Environmental studies

A study of animal families might be appropriate, particularly as Brer Rabbit is constantly talking about family connections. (See Environmental notes for *The Wind in the Willows.*)

It is worth examining the relationship of these families to each other in the wild, e.g. that of the fox and the rabbit.

Much is made of Brer Rabbit's house. What would his natural habitat be? How about his friends? A study could be made of the animals' eating habits. Which of these animals would in fact fish?

As a side issue, the subject of hunting might be discussed. Historically, wolves and bears were hunted, foxes still are. Why should this be? What are the children's feelings about this?

## Language

Much oral work could develop from the stories. Children could discuss the occasions when they, like Brer Rabbit, make excuses to avoid certain things, at home, at school and to their friends. A game could be played in which one person asks 'Would you help me with . . . ?' and another replies 'Sorry, I can't do that because . . .' This could be extended by the first person replying to the excuse with an attempt at further persuasion. The art of persuasion could be discussed and may even result in a consideration of the 'hidden persuaders' within our society.

Children could be asked to compile lists of animal metaphors, e.g. as strong as a . . . , as weak as a . . . , etc. Work could also be done on 'Mighty Big Talk'. Lists of superlatives found in the stories could be made and added to. They might then be asked to write a speech extolling their own virtues as in an electoral address or in an interview before a sporting event, etc. Stories could be written about how they managed to trick someone into leaving their house. What means could be employed?

## Art

A model of Brer Rabbit's house could be made.

Many complex and beautiful patterns are found in the considerable variety of turtle shells – the children could be

shown illustrations of these and then encouraged to devise
their own patterns based on this shape.

# Further Reading

## Non-fiction

**Animal Families** (Macdonald: World About Us)

**Wild Creatures of the British Isles** (Starfish Books)
*G. Mandley*

## Fiction

**Brer Rabbit and Brer Fox** (Collins)
*Joel Chandler Harris*

**Brer Rabbit Stories** (BBC Publications: Jackanory)

**Shadrach** (Collins)
*M. Dejong*

**The Lion and Other Animal Stories** (BBC Publications:
Jackanory)

**Watership Down** (Puffin)
*Richard Adams*
Heroic saga about wild rabbits establishing a new warren.
Contains much rabbit mythology. Ideal for reading to the class.
Winner of the 1973 Guardian Award and the Carnegie Medal.

# Children of the New Forest

*Captain Marryat*

Children will find this book an exciting tale of adventure and courage. A study of the historical and environmental references made in the text should enrich the children's understanding and enjoyment of the story.

## Topic: England at the time of the Civil War

An historical investigation might include areas such as the political context, costume, housing, transport, disease, food and weapons.

Political background: What is meant by Civil War? Why were the King and Parliament fighting? Who were the main protagonists?

Housing: Houses of the rich such as Arnwood could be contrasted with the dwellings of the poor i.e. the forester's cottage. This will inevitably raise the question of differing life styles, use of servants and their status etc.

Disease: Reference is made to smallpox in the story. The plague and other diseases were common. A contrast could be made with our modern knowledge and resources for combating disease.

Transport: The horse was the only form of transport, roads were poor. What effects did this have on communications and the war itself?

Food: References to food in the text could be followed up by research into diet, the differences between the eating habits of rich and poor, agriculture and hunting.

Weapons: Edward wears the family sword. Cannon and muskets also featured in the Civil War. Parliament's victory was largely attributable to the emergence of a properly trained army for the first time in English history.

## Topic: The New Forest

The theme of forests would also make an interesting area of study. Royal hunting forests developed from the time of William the Conqueror. Ancient laws and customs could be studied. What was hunted? How was the game protected? What rights did the commoner have? The New Forest offers a rich and varied habitat for a variety of flora and fauna from large mammals such as the ponies and deer to rare butterflies and moths. Finally the question of what has happened to these huge tracts of wooded land which once covered so much of England could be raised.

## Language

The concepts of trust, loyalty, honesty and bravery feature in the story. Discussion of these could lead to the children giving examples to show their understanding of these concepts.

Historical research and imagination might be fused in diary writing. Children could imagine that they are one of the protagonists and write a diary around the events of the story. This could be extended into the future hinted at in the last chapter.

## Art

The costumes of the period could be depicted in collage with, for example, papier doilies for lace collars and cuffs, thin strips of paper curled for the Cavalier wigs and foil paper for the Roundhead armour etc. The Arnwood children could be shown in their normal attire and that of their disguise as forest children. Children will be interested to see paintings of the period especially if a visit to see originals can be arranged.

## Further Reading

### Non-fiction

**Oliver Cromwell** (Ladybird Series)

**The Early Stuarts and the Civil War** (Longman)
*Viola Bailey and Ella Wise*

**The English Civil War** (Jonathan Cape: Jackdaws)

**Tudors and Stuarts** (A. & C. Black)
*R. J. Unstead*

**The Nature Trail Book of Trees and Leaves** (Usborne)

### Fiction

**Children of the New Forest**
*Captain Marryat*

**Brendon Chase** (Methuen)
*B.B.*

# Chitty-Chitty-Bang-Bang

*Ian Fleming*

The hero of this story is undoubtedly the car, not any car but a car that changes into a boat and an aeroplane.

## Topic: Transport

By examining the changes in the car one could begin to define the characteristics of different modes of transport. Thus:

| Car | Boat | Aeroplane |
|---|---|---|
| Land | Water | Air |
| Steering wheel | Rudder | Joystick, etc. |

In the modern world, there are special rules of the road, sea and air. There are sea lanes and air corridors as well as roads. Restrictions are imposed by traffic lights and speed limits and warnings given by signs. How are warnings given at sea? (Note the clues given on page 28 of the book.) How are contacts maintained with aeroplanes and ships: how do they find their way?

Many boys would enjoy a detailed examination of the car. Starting points for this work can be found on pages 13, 16, 17 and 18 of the book, where lights, windscreen and wipers, speedometers, radiator, petrol and horn are mentioned. A history of the motor car could be attempted. Many boys are particularly interested in motor racing and military adaptations of the car such as the jeep.

Finally, of course, a topic on transport gives the teacher an ideal opportunity to discuss safety aspects for both motorists and pedestrians. The Green Cross Code could be discussed, and road safety officers and policemen can be invited into the school to talk to the children.

## Language

On page 22 of the book Jemima says 'I can see the sea. We are going over the sea and over all the little ships on the sea.' The idea of the bird's eye view can be expanded and used as a basis for stories and poems. 'Imagine you are flying on a magic carpet, that you have changed into a bird, or that you are looking down from a high mountain.' The idea is the opposite to that of magnification and this can be pointed out to the children – 'what happens when you look through the wrong end of a telescope?'

Children respond to the idea of catching burglars. This response could be developed and connected with art work. Wanted posters of the burglars in the story could be designed, full descriptions of their appearance written and outlines of their careers made. The various pieces of work could be displayed together as a Rogues Gallery.

Commander Pott is an inventor. The children can pretend to be inventors and design and describe their own inventions, e.g. invent a machine that does the washing up, makes a cup of tea and cleans the kitchen floor all at the same time.

## Drama

Improvisations can be based on situations in the story. Children would enjoy being burglars, plotting in their cave perhaps or 'out on the job'. The drama of being trapped by the tide whilst on a picnic would provide a good stimulus. (For full treatment of this theme, see the Drama section of notes on *The Wind in the Willows.*)

## Mathematics

The incident in Bon-Bon's shop could lead to work on codes and secret messages dealing perhaps with a simple code such as A = 1, B = 2, etc. The children would find the necessity for special signs to show the ends of words and sentences. More complex codes can be devised using mathematical shapes or processes, e.g. for E = 5 substitute E = (2 + 3), for F = 6 substitute F = (3 + 3), etc. By this means a code is devised and number bonds are reinforced at the same time.

Children will also be interested in making messages pricked onto paper with a pin. Lemon juice will act as invisible ink which becomes visible on being heated.

## Art

Models of various forms of transport can be made. Junk and collected materials can be used creatively by younger children, while older children should be able to use Balsa wood and clay for more representational models. Collage pictures can be made using magazine pictures of cars, etc. The Wanted posters (see Language section) may be simply painted or made more interesting by the addition of other materials: an eye patch added cut out of black felt, moustaches, beards and hair made from string and wool, etc.

Inventions can be made from collected materials such as wire and string, and then displayed with the accompanying written work.

# Further Reading

## Non-fiction

**Car Racing** (Nelson: Lively Readers)
*Leonard Sealey*

**Henry Ford** (Macdonald: Starters People)

**The Aeroplane** (Ladybird)

**The Locomotive** (Ladybird)

**The Motor Car** (Macdonald: Junior Reference Library)

**The Ocean Liner** (Ladybird)

**The Wright Brothers** (Macdonald: Starters People)

## Fiction

**Bedknob and Broomstick** (Puffin)
*Mary Norton*
Charles, Paul and Carey happened to know how Miss Price hurt her ankle – by falling off a broomstick! So she cast a spell on Paul's bedknob.

**Chitty-Chitty-Bang-Bang** (Pan)
*Ian Fleming*

**My Friend Mr Leakey** (Puffin)
*J. B. S. Haldane*
Mr Leakey was a practical magician. He could do such useful things as bringing a sock to life and bewitching tie-pins and diaries so he would never lose them. He could also use a touch of invisibility to cure a dog that was always biting people.

**The Furious Flycycle** (Puffin)
*Jan Wahl*
Richly humorous story about a brainbox called Melvin Spitznagle and his brilliant discovery of a machine to make his bicycle fly.

# The Family from One End Street

*Eve Garnett*

This story of the joys and tribulations of urban family life in the 1930's is most entertaining as well as being very true to life.

## Topic: Family life

A comparative study could be made of the Ruggles' family life in the 1930's and that of the pupils. There are various clues in the text, for example washing by hand, the aspidistra, the 11+, the baby show, the silk petticoat, the house itself, etc, to suggest immediate differences. Pupils could be encouraged to do their own research at home by questioning parents and grandparents about their childhood and then report their findings to the class. Photographs and magazine pictures could be displayed.

The Ruggles appear to be a happy family despite all their worries and the children might like to consider how they can contribute to their own family life.

## Language

The children could write their own autobiographies starting from babyhood as a follow-up to the chapter on the baby show. Chapter headings might include 'Why I was called . . .', 'My first day at school', 'A family outing' etc.

Form filling could be attempted if the teacher prepares a questionnaire related to the children's interests and hobbies. A collection could be made of well-known sayings which Mrs Ruggles is so fond of using as well as others not in the text. These could be displayed with illustrations showing literally what is said along with an explanation of their actual meanings.

The children could practise their own letter writing, preferably by writing letters, for example, to an organization requesting information needed for project work or to the Headmaster describing the work being followed in class. The point is that the letters should be actually sent.

## Mathematics

The children might like to consider how they would have spent the reward money with their families and to write down an account of how it was used. They could be given experience of budgeting a sum of money, for example, they might imagine they were to feed the Ruggles family for one meal. Food could be drawn on the blackboard and priced and the children given a fixed sum to spend.

Local bus and train fares could be consulted to see how much it would cost five children and two adults to make local journeys. How much would it have cost the Ruggles to go to London from the children's home town?

Information about the children's families, for example, numbers in families, types of living accommodation, etc, could be displayed as histograms.

## Art

A frieze could be made of a street with each child contributing a building. The windows and doors of each building could open to reveal the behind scenes of the families and people within. Speech bubbles could be drawn and conversations shown. Shops and offices could also be included. The time of day might be agreed upon beforehand to give continuity to the scene. People in the street might also be shown talking. A train journey could be treated in a similar way with the inside of the compartments being shown. Young children often have difficulty in drawing people and might like to try tearing the shape of a person from newspaper and then folding and sticking them into the appropriate positions.

## Drama

Small groups could improvise scenes around family life. Themes might include 'Breakfast time', 'A shopping trip', 'A family outing'. Alternatively, with a larger group a 'Visit to London' could be used as a theme.

## Further Reading

(See also Further Reading for **The Treasure Seekers**.)

## Non-fiction

**The Twentieth Century**
*R. J. Unstead*

## Fiction

**Further Adventures of the Family from One End Street** (Puffin)
*Eve Garnett*

**Little House in the Big Woods** and other Little House books (Puffin)
*Laura Ingalls Wilder*

# Flat Stanley
*Jeff Brown*

Children enjoy the adventures of a little boy who wakes up one morning to find that he is no longer three-dimensional like his brother Arthur. His changed relationship with his environment – the source of much of the humour of the book – can be highlighted with a mathematical treatment taking as the starting point Dr Dan's measurements of Stanley on page 16 of the book.

## Topic: Mathematics

A chart could be made to show Stanley's measurements and this compared with the child's own. The child's own chart might be drawn up as follows:

My height is . . . metres
The length of my leg is . . . centimetres
The length of my arm is . . . centimetres
The length of my hand is . . . centimetres
The length of my foot is . . . centimetres
The width of my hand is . . . centimetres
The width of my foot is . . . centimetres
The distance round my head is . . . centimetres

Measurement can be linked with work on area, e.g. 'You have measured yourself, now find out how much surface you cover when you lie down. Ask your friends to draw round you.' This area could be covered by non-standard measures such as building bricks or, at a more advanced level, the outline could be drawn on squared paper.

Stanley's peculiarity is his 'thinness'. Discussion of this leads naturally to work on two- and three-dimensional shapes, and thus to volume. The children could look for hollow containers which are two centimetres thick like Stanley, e.g. matchboxes, and find out what quantities of given materials are needed to fill them. Further practical work making three-dimensional shapes such as cubes and tetrahedrons would help reinforce the concepts involved.

Stanley is described as being 'as flat as a pancake' – the child could be asked to search for other mathematical metaphors, e.g. as high as a . . . , as wide as a . . . , etc.

## Language

Stanley's journey in an envelope could serve as a stimulus for creative writing. The children might be asked to imagine what it would be like to travel by such means. What did Stanley hear and feel? What would it be like to travel in a similar way, e.g. in a matchbox or in someone's pocket? Reference could be made to Gulliver and Tom Thumb.

Many children will sympathize with Arthur's role in the story. The idea of jealousy between siblings could be discussed, and the children encouraged to write about their own experiences of such feelings. Also the role of the parent can be introduced, with special attention paid to parental remonstrances such as 'Don't keep shouting, Hey! Hay is for horses not people.'

## Drama

Certain situations in the story such as the burglary are ideal for dramatic improvisation. Children in groups could form Art Gallery tableaux and then bring them to life. The teacher might introduce this idea by showing the children famous 'group' paintings such as *Interior* by Pieter de Hooch, and asking the children to interpret what is happening.

## Art

The making of kites would be an interesting art topic. Traditional kite motifs such as those of the Japanese and the discussion of the ritual uses of kites would be an enriching experience, culminating in the actual flying of the kites made.

As a link with the dramatic work the children can make their own Portrait Gallery – including tableaux – with collage materials and sticky paper as well as paint. Frames could be made with paper or foil.

Puppets of Stanley could be made out of thin card hinged together at the joints with paper fasteners or cotton.


# Further Reading

## Non-fiction

**Kites** (Collins: Make it Easy Books)

**Kites** (Macdonald: Starters Science)

## Fiction

**Down to Earth** (Puffin)
*Patricia Wrightson*
To start with, no one believed that Martin came from outer space; but what was the explanation of his green glow, his

ability to squeeze into the smallest spaces, or the way he bounced?

**Flat Stanley** (Puffin)
*Jeff Brown and Tomi Ungerer*

Illustration from Flat Stanley

# The Land of Oz

*L. Frank Baum*

The appeal of the stories about the Land of Oz lies largely in the fantasy world which the author has created. Both the environment and the characters who inhabit it are the products of an imagination to which children readily respond.

## Topic: A fantasy world

Children will enjoy the opportunity of creating a fantasy world of their own. As a starting point a three-dimensional model of an imaginary kingdom could be built from newspaper and lint soaked in plaster of paris. Towns, rivers, mountains and other geographical features will need to be named and labelled. Stories can then be written about the kingdom and its inhabitants. Dangers and adversities may affect the inhabitants and some of these will form suitable themes for dramatic work.

## Language

In the story the little boy, Tip, has some of the magic powder. Children could think about what they would like to bring to life if they possessed this powder – perhaps a favourite toy, doll or ornament. Adventure stories could be written featuring themselves and the objects they choose.

The children could look at the differences between the characters in the story. Which would they prefer to be? What could/couldn't they do? What could harm them? What faculties do they consider to be most important? The importance of friendship is stressed throughout. What is it that they like about their friends? Can they define the word 'friend'? Examples of homonyms appear in the text on page 30 and could be used as a starting point for the class's own collection of homonyms.

In a similar vein a list of abbreviations could be compiled taking as a starting point the discussion on page 39 of the story.

## Mathematics

Discussion on pages 56 and 61 of the story focuses on counting in 2s. Children could investigate why it is difficult to count to 17 in 2s. What is the difference between odd and even numbers?

Most of the characters in the story have two legs but Saw-Horse has 4 and Woggle-Bug has 6. Can the children think of other creatures with 4, 6, 8 and more than 8 legs? Practise in number bonds and facts can be based round their findings, for example: how many legs would 5 Woggle-Bugs have? etc.

Number puzzles could be collected such as 'Think of a number, but don't tell me what it is. Double it. Add 6. Halve it. Take away the number you first thought of. Your answer is 3'. Magic squares might also be introduced.

## Art

'Contrast' tables could be set up, showing silver and green objects as suggested by the Emerald and Silver cities. Three-dimensional models could be made from boxes covered in silver foil, foil containers, milk bottle tops etc. Patterns could be imprinted on the foil with pencils. Tinted glasses are worn in the Emerald city. Children could make their own glasses and experiment with lenses made from different coloured stage lighting gels or tissue paper. This could be extended to work on the primary colours using prisms and the making of colour wheels. There are obvious links here with science which can be explored, for example: what happens to plants which are kept in the dark?

The Woggle-Bug is a little insect highly magnified. Scale and magnification are important ideas in art and children will have already discussed scale when building their magic city. They might now experiment by drawing on small pieces of squared paper and then enlarging the squares onto larger pieces of paper and plotting the drawings. Much incidental maths work will take place during this activity.

## Further Reading

(See also Further Reading for **The Wizard of Oz**.)

## Non-Fiction

**Insects** (The Clue Books: Oxford University Press)

**Light, Mirrors and Lenses** (Ladybird)

## Fiction

**James and the Giant Peach** (Penguin)
*Roald Dahl*

**Adventures of the Little Wooden Horse** (Penguin)
*U. M. Williams*

# The Last of the Mohicans

*James Fenimore Cooper*

This story of Indian life is set in the Eastern woodlands of
Canada at a time in history when the Canadian nation was
being forged. The influence of the white man on Indian life is
apparent. If children read this in conjunction with Beaverbird
(see page 12) they will have a more than adequate starting
point for a topic on Indians.

## Topic: Canadian Indians

The Indian tribes of the region could be investigated under
the following headings:

Tribes: The Hurons and the Delawares are just two of many
woodland tribes whose domain stretched from the St. Lawrence
and the Great Lakes to the Ohio River and the Carolinas. The
Hurons were related to the savage Iroquois. The children could
find out more about these tribes and the areas in which they
lived comparing and contrasting their life styles.

Religions: Numerous spirits were worshipped including the
Master of Light — the Supreme Being. Tribal magicians were
called Shamans. Rituals and religious beliefs involved with the
subsistence quest, the dead, curing the sick, interpersonal
relationships and divinations could be researched. Such beliefs
could be contrasted with religious beliefs in other cultures. The
topic of superstition can be particularly fruitful.

Daily Life: Most tribes were village dwellers. Their time was
divided between agriculture, hunting and fishing. Questions to
be answered might include: What crops did they grow? How
did they prepare their food? What skills were necessary for
survival? How did they build their homes? How did their
family life differ from ours?

Appearance: Most clothing was made from skins. Men wore
breechcloth shirts, leggings and moccasins. A feature noted in
the story is the shaved head with the scalplock. Women wore
skirts and jackets. Clothing was decorated with porcupine
quills and beads.

The White Man: The coming of the white man had a
devastating effect on the Indian way of life, as Magua says in
the play 'before the white man came to this land the Hurons
were happy'. Children could investigate what happened to the
life and traditions of the Indians leading up to the present day
reservations.

War: War between the French and English features in Cooper's novel and some children may like to investigate this particular historical aspect hinted at by the presence of the fort in the play.

Further areas worth exploring and referred to in the text are Education, Law and Woodcraft; see also the notes to Beaverbird on page 12 in this *Guidelines*.

## Language

Many sayings or proverbs are quoted in the story, e.g. 'You cannot set a cloud to chase the wind.' Children could list these, explain their meaning and research proverbs common in our culture. Proverbs are a form of heightened or 'charged' language similar in some ways to the language of poetry. Children could proceed from proverbs to writing their own poems or songs around themes such as 'A song to Uncas', 'Last of the Mohicans', 'A chant before Battle', 'A hunting song' etc. It would be helpful if the children read examples of such poems before writing their own. See *Junior Voices* Books 1–4.

## Drama

Many aspects of Indian life lend themselves to dramatic improvisation, for example, children could improvise a religious dance based on the Huron's feast of the dead at which the bones of an ancestor are ceremonially re-buried. The drama could centre round a Shaman, chants they had written could be used and there are obvious opportunities for work on masks and costumes.

## Art

The Indians of the Eastern woodlands decorated their clothes with quills and beads often arranged in geometric patterns. Reproductions of Indian art would serve to stimulate pattern work in painting, drawing, craft and needlework. The sign of the Tortoise would be an appropriate theme for such pattern work. Craft work could be directed towards making a three-dimensional model of an Indian village complete with longhouses and stockade, and a model of a British fort.

## Further Reading

## Non-fiction

**Red Indians** (Blackwell's Learning Library)
*T. A. Thompson*

**The Story of the Indians** (Ladybird)

**Algonkians of the Eastern Woodlands** (Royal Ontario Museum) available from the Horniman Museum, Forest Hill, London

**Junior Voices** Books 1–4 (Penguin)

**Wounded Knee** (Teacher's Reference) (Chatto and Windus)
*Dee Brown*

# Fiction

**The Last of the Mohicans**
*J. Fenimore Cooper*

**Ishi, Last of his Tribe** (Puffin)
Theodore Kroeber

**The Time of the Indian** (Puffin)
*Kenneth Hyatt*

# The Merry Adventures of Robin Hood

*Howard Pyle*

Nearly every child knows and loves the myth of Robin Hood. What is rather surprising however is that the basic tales of how Little John, Friar Tuck and Midge the Miller's Son came to join the band are often forgotten amongst the galaxy of stories which have been added. They are no longer known to every child. But the slap-stick, practical-joke comedy in the original stories has an immediacy for children which is a real incentive to reading. It is of particular interest to boys and can stimulate much supportive work.

## Topic: Historical aspects

A study of feudal England examining the social structure – king, nobles, the Church, officials such as the sheriff, and the common people. Discussion of this structure should highlight the division between the rich and the poor and help to explain Robin's position and motives. Many children will already know of the story of Richard the Lionheart. It may be appropriate to mention the reasons for his absence from England – the Crusades and his other adventures.

The idea of a band of outlaws living in the forest can be explored. What are outlaws? How do they live? What would it be like living in the forest through the changing seasons of the year?

Central to the story, for boys especially, are the arms used. The longbow, broad sword and staff can be used as starting points for work on arms and armour. The development of the long bow through to its devastating use at the Battle of Crècy will interest older boys. Castles and fortified cities, such as Nottingham, can also be investigated.

Food and drink feature in the story and these could be considered in the light of cooking in the open air. The place of venison will need to be commented on, and a reference could be made to the harshness of the Game Laws of the time.

## Language

The moral aspects of the story, in particular the issue of 'robbing the rich to feed the poor', could be discussed. How would you feel if you were a rich man or, alternatively, a poor man? Was Robin justified in his actions? Was it fair? With older children, one might proceed to discuss contemporary social problems.

Robin's encounter with strangers who are later to become his friends can be paralleled with the children's own experiences of making friends. Social groups such as the family, clubs, gangs and classes might be the subject of discussion. Again, for older children parallels could be drawn between the appearance of Robin's band, i.e. all in Lincoln Green, and uniformity of dress in other social groups, e.g. the gang. Reference could be made to clothes as a distinguishing feature of a personality, and the idea of disguise explored.

All Robin's men have nicknames which refer to personal characteristics, and children could be asked to invent such names for themselves and their friends.

## Drama

Older children, especially boys, are sometimes inhibited in their drama work. However, confidence can sometimes be gained and inhibitions lost if the work is seen to involve special skills. The story of Robin Hood includes many fights and provides an opportunity for the teacher to work with the type of child referred to, on stage fighting.

An exploration of the technique of falling can be allied to PE work. The stressing of safety in practice fights encourages a discipline with a reason. As preliminary work, the children could work in pairs with one child moving and the other shadowing his movements. Quick and slow movements, turns and balance and freezing the action can all be stressed. The final fights could be in slow motion or in the convention of looking realistic with physical contact never actually being made.

A drama can then be worked round the fights rather than the reverse. As can be seen, many elements of a movement lesson are incorporated without the child being aware of them, and thus self-conscious.

## Mathematics

An early form of measurement mentioned in the story is that of using the unit of a finger's width. If this concept interests the children, an exploration of the history of measurement would be appropriate. It may also be helpful in clarifying the principles of our own system of measurement.

An ideal starting point for talking about non-standard units of measurement is the child's own body. A chart could be made of the parts of the body which can easily be used for measurement – feet, hands, fingers, arms, etc. Terms such as span can be introduced and the growth of standard measurements like the foot examined. Children should be led to realize that non-standard measurements based on the body vary from person to person and come to understand for themselves the need for standard measurement.

A discussion of fractions would be helpful in the understanding of the references in the text, i.e. ⅓ of £1500 and ½ of £50.

# Art

There are many good subjects for paintings in the story especially the fights, feasts with the Bishop and the Sheriff, the archery competition, the rescue of Will Scarlet and the unmasking of King Richard.

The idea of the camouflage of Lincoln Green can be incorporated into a group frieze. A background of the forest could be painted and made, leaves cut out of material and attached, figures painted separately and then cut out and stuck on. The outlaws could be painted green and hidden in the trees and undergrowth waiting in ambush. Other figures representing those about to be ambushed could be added. Children will enjoy seeing whose outlaw is most difficult to pick out.

The circular shape of the targets used in modern archery could form the basis of colour wheels. Experimentation with colour blends and contrasts on a spinning disc might follow.

# Further Reading

## Non-fiction

### A Book of Heroes (Puffin)
*Selected by William Mayne*
A hero has some quality which makes him slightly larger than life, and slightly larger than death too. Here are all sorts of heroes from Sir Francis Drake and Sir Richard Grenville to Volund the cripple.

### Castles (Macdonald: Starters Long Ago)

### Hero Tales from the British Isles (Puffin)
*Barbara Leonie Picard*
Romantic and rousing stories of the heroes and warriors of Britain.

### King Arthur and his Knights of the Round Table (Puffin)
*Roger Lancelyn Green*
The old stories of chivalry told afresh from the original sources, with beautiful scissor-cut pictures by Lotte Reiniger. (Original)

### Knights and the Crusades (Macdonald: Toppers History)

**Living in a Castle** (A. & C. Black)
*R. J. Unstead*

**Richard the Lionheart** (Ladybird)

**The Middle Ages** (A. & C. Black)
*R. J. Unstead*

**Weapons and Armour** (Macdonald: Starters Long Ago)

# Fiction

**Robin Hood** (BBC Publications: Jackanory)
*Edward Blishen*

**The Adventures of Robin Hood** (Puffin)
*Roger Lancelyn Green*
The tale of Robin Hood and his merry men in Sherwood
Forest, which never ceases to fire the imagination. (Original)

**The Ambush** (Ladybird)

**The Merry Adventures of Robin Hood** (Dover
Publications)
*Howard Pyle*

**The Silver Arrow** (Ladybird)

# Mystery at Black Pony Inn

*Christine Pullein-Thompson*

Mystery at Black Pony Inn, an exciting story of kidnapping and adventure with a strong equestrian flavour, will appeal equally to boys and girls.

## Topic: Horses

The story is full of references to horses and riding and these can be used as starting points for further study. What, for example, is the difference between a horse and a pony? What are the various parts of a horse called? What equipment is used in riding? What do horses eat? etc.

Children may well be interested to learn about the evolution of the horse from its forefather, Eohippus. The horse has played an important part in man's history in war, agriculture, and as a means of transport. There are still some working horses but in general children will be more familiar with the horse in the context of recreation, for example, racing, show jumping, hunting and pony trekking.

## Language

Most children will have seen reports of kidnapping on television or read about them in newspapers. The idea of media coverage can be used to provide both oral and written language work. Newspaper and television reports of the rescue incorporating eye witness accounts and interviews with the protagonists could be produced. Children could study news reports and produce their writing in column form complete with suitable headlines.

Oral and written work coupled with reading reinforcement will be obtained if children work in pairs producing their own take part version of Paul and Commander Cooley's ride. Added interests will be generated by listening to each other's version and comparing solutions to the mystery of the gash on Cassandra's shoulder.

## Mathematics

Several geographical locations in the story are mentioned between pages 45–55. Children could draw these onto squared paper using their own or conventional symbols, including a key giving the grid reference for each symbol. Alternatively, the teacher could read out grid references on which she wishes the symbols to be placed.

There is specific reference to time in the story. Children could revise their time telling and possibly devise a time table for a day at Black Pony Inn.

## Drama

Reference is made at the end of the story to the impending trial of Commander Cooley. The trial could form the basis of an improvised drama. The characters in the story will need to give evidence. As well as a policeman, there should be a judge, lawyers, witnesses and a jury. The link between more formal language work and drama can be made if children prepare their statements before the trial. This will, of course, require careful re-reading of the text and thus incidental reading reinforcement.

Alternatively, the idea of a rescue makes a fruitful theme. This need not be Paul but could be a character, or characters in a similar desperate situation. Rescues sometimes involve some degree of violence and this will provide teachers with a chance to introduce the idea of mime, slow motion and the discipline of stage fighting.

## Art

Children could study a newspaper photograph with a hand lens so that they can see that the picture is made up of tiny dots. They could then produce their own 'Scoop' photograph using the technique of working with tiny dots and black and white. An extension of this work would be to look at some examples of pointalism and produce full colour pictures.

# Further Reading

## Non-fiction

**My learn to ride book** (Hamlyn)

**The How and Why Wonder Book of Horses** (Transworld)

**The Book of Riding** (Arthur Barker)
*C. E. G. Hope*

**Prehistoric Life** (Macdonald)
*Ramona–Anne Gale*

## Fiction

**Come Home Brumby** (Penguin)
*M. E. Patchet*

# Parsley and the Herbs

*Michael Bond*

The story of Parsley is a great favourite with many children who will have seen some of his adventures on television. As an introduction to the Take Part version, it may well be a good idea to plant some herbs in pots in the classroom, thereby making a miniature herb garden. Seeds are easily available from gardening shops.

Because of the nature of these stories, it is probably easier to deal with each one in turn rather than under umbrella headings.

## Parsley's Tail

This, the first story, centres around Parsley losing his tail. Discussion of Parsley's predicament might be extended into discussion of the importance of tails to other animals and birds, e.g. the prehensile tails of some monkeys, the eyed tail of the peacock and the tail-less Manx cat.

## Parsley's Good Deed

The idea of a good deed which has unfortunate consequences will be familiar to many children and may provoke discussion of their own personal experiences particularly in the home.

The idea of the catapult is introduced in this story. Children may well be interested in the uses of the catapult through the ages. The story of David and Goliath could be told. The medieval use of giant catapults for hurling fire or huge stones in siege warfare could be mentioned. A modern example of the use of the catapult is in the launching of planes from aircraft carriers.

## Parsley's Problem Present

Children enjoy talking about their birthdays, favourite presents and toys. A survey of class birthdays could be made and a chart or graph drawn up showing the frequency of birthdays in each month.

The problem of hat size could be discussed. How can you find the size of your head? The children could measure their own heads using pieces of string, which could then be mounted side by side on card to make a graph of head sizes. Some experimental work on water displacement could be carried out in the water tray, bowl or sink.

## Language

Sage's present is going to be a Balaclava. The children will already be familiar with different types of hats. The idea of having a magic hat could provide the stimulus for imaginative writing. The hat could either change its wearer unexpectedly or, at their request, into another shape, or make them invisible and so on. The stories could tell the wearer's adventures.

## Drama
The idea of the 'magic' hat could be extended in drama work. You have a magic hat, put it on – now you are as tall as a giant, now you can fly, now you are as tiny as an ant, etc. A parade of hats made as suggested in the Art section, could make an enjoyable class activity.

## Art
Animals with useful or unusual tails would make good subjects for paintings. A peacock's tail could be made out of collage. Foil paper or sticky coloured paper or tissue is particularly effective for the 'eyes' of the tail.

A frieze of the Herb Garden could be made showing all the characters, including other flowers and plants.

The practical work on head sizes can be utilized in the making of hats. These can be made from card or thick paper, glued or stapled together. The children will find that some hats require a more exact fit than others. They could make crowns, helmets, witches' and wizards' hats, Easter bonnets, stove pipe hats, etc.

# Further Reading

## Non-fiction
**Growing Things Indoors** (Macdonald Starters)

**Indoor Gardening** (Ladybird)

## Fiction
**Parsley Parade** (Collins: Armada Lions)
*Michael Bond*

**Parsley's Problem Present** (BBC Publications)
*Michael Bond*

**Parsley the Lion** (Collins: Armada Lions)
*Michael Bond*

# Six Folk Tales

*Leila Berg*

Good folk tales are acceptable to people of all ages, and children do not seem to need much persuasion to read Leila Berg's original when they are able to. The simple approach of these tales seemed to lend itself bewitchingly well for use in Take Part form by children who have only broken through the earliest stages of reading. It is a good introduction to the Take Part method, making full use of repetition and rhythms in speech and is intended for children at the 6 to 8 reading level, with several parts at the 7-year-old level. The variety of stories helps to keep attention in these very early days. The interest in humour and trickery which children show when reading these tales could well spill over into follow-up work. Language and artwork stem naturally from this source.

## Language

The ideas of trickery and food feature largely in these tales, and can be used to advantage in language enrichment work. The Soup-Stone and Anansi and the Pudding Tree lend themselves to discussion and written work about food. The element of fantasy in the Pudding Tree could be extended.

The children might be asked to invent other sources of food, e.g. the sausage plant or the cornflakes bush. They could be asked to describe the taste of the puddings so eagerly sought by Anansi. An extension of the idea into simple phonic work might concentrate on giving food characteristics, e.g. 'angry apples', 'bashful bananas'. The alliterative element in this approach lends itself to development in poetry.

In The Soup-Stone, the stone itself is an obviously ridiculous ingredient in the recipe. Discussion of the ideas of recipes, familiar to many children through their cooking activities, can be developed into the invention of recipes containing ridiculous ingredients. The children's imaginative powers can be called upon into thinking of humorous, gruesome and unusual ingredients. What might the foods taste like? They could be medicines, magic potions or foods for unusual people, e.g. gods, giants and ogres.

In Anansi and the Pudding Tree, the spider is referred to as Ceiling Thomas, as in Brer Rabbit the terrapin is called Old Shellyback. Animals have distinctive features which can serve as clues for nicknames. What nickname could you invent for a camel, a sloth, a worm, etc.

The mouse does not say Anansi's name, but we know to whom

he is speaking. The children could write poems or descriptive passages giving clues as to identity without mentioning the actual name as in Anglo Saxon riddle poems or *Prayers from the Ark* translated by Rumer Godden.

## Drama

In The Woman who Always Argued, the ideas of contradiction and argument are central. These are essentially dramatic and much oral work could develop from this theme. Children's improvisation could begin with the idea of opposites, perhaps in large groups, e.g.

Yes – No
Right – Left,

then in smaller groups and pairs contradicting each other, e.g.

The sun is coming up –
No it's not, it's going down.

The whole group could then improvise a drama around a disagreement or argument. Written work should be enriched by this sort of dramatic activity.

## Art

A frieze or large picture of strange food plants, perhaps a magic food garden, would follow naturally from the written work.

The animals in the stories could be modelled in clay, paper-mâché or other materials. Anansi, for example, might be made from clay with pipe cleaners bent for legs, or more interestingly from a 'found' object such as a large fir cone. The 'stripy monster' of the Elephant would look good made from collage.

A large painting of the Horse with all his passengers, painted according to the details given on page 61 of the book, could involve a group of children.

## Further Reading

### Fiction

**Annancy Stories** (Ginn: Beacon Library)

**First (and Second) Book of Fairy Tales** (Collins: Armada Lions)
*retold by Helen Cresswell*

**Jack Stories** (BBC Publications: Jackanory)

**Six Folk Tales** (Brockhampton Press)
*Leila Berg*

# Space Hostages
*Nicholas Fisk*

Space Hostages is an exciting science fiction adventure and as
such serves as an ideal starting point for work on space and space
flight.

## Topic: Space

Children could begin by investigating the space explorations
of the last few years. How are astronauts chosen? What sort of
training do they have? What types of craft do they travel in?
Concepts such as air pressure, gravitational pull, orbit and
cosmic dust can be covered in work on the planets and the
universe.

The development of the rocket-powered flight makes a
fascinating study. One of the problems of rocket technology
has always been that of fuel consumption and this leads naturally
to discussion of nuclear engines, nuclear energy and radiation.

## Mathematics

Children will be familiar with the way that hands move round a clock
face and will have heard of compasses. These basic experiences can be
used as starting points for introducing the idea of rotating first
themselves and then other objects through a circle and of measuring
these turns in the standard unit of degrees. Simple vector work will
follow naturally from these experiences.

## Language

In the story Brylo is talked down to earth by radio. It is often
quite difficult to follow verbal instructions and the giving and
receiving of these is a valuable experience in oracy. Children
can work in pairs across a table visually screened from one
another. Each partner can have an identical set of objects – for
example Unifix cubes. One partner performs an action and
instructs the other to do the same. After several actions have been
completed the final results are compared. They should of course
be identical. Tasks can be increased in complexity to correspond
to the verbal skills of the children involved.

Creative writing could be based on themes such as 'A dream
come true', 'Lost in Space', 'Adventure on the Moon', 'Moon
Creatures'.

## Drama

A Space Adventure lends itself to dramatic improvisation.
The Astronauts prepare, board the space craft, adjust the controls

and take off. The hazards of the journey over, they land on a strange planet and experience weightlessness. Scientific investigations are interrupted by strange aliens. The astronauts escape from their terrifying predicament and return to a tumultuous reception on earth. The story will be enhanced if electronic music is used to give added atmosphere to the drama.

## Music

Music such as *The Planet Suite* by Holst and *Thus spake Zarathustra* by Strauss can be played as a stimulus for creative writing and art work. Listening to examples of electronic music will help make the children aware of the possibilities of creative music making. Using percussion instruments the story of a space journey could be told in sound.

## Art

Space communications and space ship controls are featured in the story. Children enjoy working in three dimensions and they could create a control and communications console out of cardboard boxes. Dials and switches could be made from bottle tops and cane. A movable switch surrounded by a dial marked in degrees would provide mathematical reinforcement and the finished console will stimulate much incidental language reinforcement, especially if various dials, switches and levers are labelled.

## Science

Simple telephones can be made from tin cans linked by string. Children could also make a simple electrical circuit using a battery which rings a buzzer when the circuit is closed. The apparatus can then be used to send morse code messages. A more sophisticated version of the machine could include a light bulb to flash on and off giving a visual signal to correspond to the audible one.

## Further Reading

### Non-fiction

**The Night Sky** (Ladybird)

**How It Works: The Rocket** (Ladybird)

**The Story of Nuclear Power** (Ladybird)

**The Young Scientist's Book of Space Flight** (Usborne)

**Your Book of Space Travel** (Faber)
*D. M. Desoutter*

# Stories from Grimm

The familiar always has an appeal for children and they will approach the Take Part version of these tales with enthusiasm and confidence, both vital factors in the early stages of reading. This book could also serve as a starting point for re-readings of other familiar fairy tales from Grimm and Anderson. Many of these stories lend themselves to dramatization and a culminating point could be a dramatic production of a festival of fairy tales (for a more detailed treatment of this idea see Lane and Kemp's *An Approach to Creative Writing in the Primary School*).

## Language

Food plays an important part in Hansel and Gretel and Briar Rose. How was the Gingerbread House decorated? What might have been served at the Christening party? Children could compile their own lists of favourite foods, sweet and savoury foods etc. A tasting competition could be held with children being blindfolded as they taste a variety of foods, the object being to describe the different tastes and if possible to identify them correctly. An edible gingerbread house could be made using a cardboard model as a base. Sweets and biscuits made by the children could be stuck to the base with icing sugar. Such a model would certainly provide a talking point as well as giving practice in reading and following written recipes. Christian names are referred to in Briar Rose and Rumpelstiltskin. Children could compile their own alphabet of ordinary and extraordinary names as well as researching the meanings and derivations of their own names. The reference to 13 as an unlucky number could lead to discussion of their own superstitions. The gifts offered to Briar Rose could be examined. Which was the best gift? Is it possible to put the gifts in order of importance? Finally, children could be encouraged to find out from reference books more about spinning so that they understand the meanings of spindle, flax, spinning wheels, etc, which are mentioned in both Briar Rose and Rumpelstiltskin.

## Drama

Hansel and Gretel's plight of being lost in a forest, finding a house and meeting the witch could be taken as a starting point for group improvisation. The 'Hansel and Gretel Overture' could be used as an introduction.

The story of Briar Rose lends itself to group improvisation. The idea of the party could be developed with the preparation of the food, the cleaning of the gold plates, the laying of the tables, heralds announcing the guests, musicians playing, courtiers dancing, the feast and presentation of the gifts. As the party is sent to sleep other children could improvise the briar rose growing with the subsequent arrival of the prince. Percussive instruments could be used to evoke the moods throughout.

## Art

A large fairy-tale frieze could be made from paint and collage depicting the events from a variety of fairy tales. Small groups of children could be responsible for each story. The characters shown in the frieze could be identified by speech bubbles showing appropriate phrases. Much oral work could extend from such a frieze with children telling the stories aloud to each other.

# Further Reading

## Non-fiction

**An Approach to Creative Writing in the Primary School** (Blackie)
*Sheila Lane and Marion Kemp*

**Cakes and Biscuits** (Macdonald Starters Activities)

**Sweetmaking for Children** (Piccolo)
*Margaret Powell*

**A First Look at Cloth** (Franklin Watts)
*R. Kerrod*

**Name Your Child** (Summit Paperback)
*Eric Partridge*

## Fiction

**Grimms Fairy Tales** (Piccolo)

**Sleeping Beauty** (Ladybird Easy Readers)

**Rumpelstiltskin** (Ladybird Easy Readers)

# Treasure Island

*Robert Louis Stevenson*

Treasure Island, one of the classics of children's literature, is a tale of danger and adventure centred round the sea. A project on life at sea in the eighteenth century could be undertaken drawing on several strands mentioned in the story.

## Topic: Life at sea in the 18th century

Ships: This was the age of the sailing ship. Children could trace the development of the sailing ship. They could look at the oared galleys of the Mediterranean area, the great Elizabethan fighting ships, the finer designs of the Dutch and the English in the Navy of Samuel Pepys, leading up to the tall clippers renowned for their grace and speed. Names for the parts of ships could be learned.

Sailors: The sailor's life was incredibly hard. Rations, types of jobs, the composition of the crew, pay, sleeping arrangements, disease and the press gang all provide fruitful areas of investigation.

Pirates: An additional hazard of the seas was that of pirates and privateers. Tracing the development of privateers would bring in the lives of many famous seamen from Sir Henry Morgan to Paul Jones. A study of pirates could include a look at the Spanish Main and at things more popularly associated with pirates such as the skull and crossbones, walking the plank, etc.

## Language

Many words in common everyday use are derived from nautical vocabulary. Children could compile lists of words referring to ships and the sea, and phrases and sayings associated with sailors and pirates, e.g. 'sailing close to the wind', 'walking the plank', etc.

There are many accounts of life at sea from which teachers could read extracts. After there has been sufficient time for their own research, children could be asked to write their own diary or journal of life at sea. This could take the form of a journal of their own treasure hunt. They would need to invent their own treasure island, complete with hazards, as well as dramatic personae. The journal could tell how the treasure map was found, describe the voyage made and relate the difficulties overcome ending, perhaps, with a description of the treasure eventually found.

## Mathematics

A mathematical topic could hinge on map work. Children could be introduced to simple compass work, the idea of right angle turns and then of bearings. They could make their own cardboard compass. Map work would bring in practice in using grid references. The teacher could draw an island with features inside a square grid and then ask the children to read off the grid references of key features. This could be extended to children working in pairs, one placing features on an outline map at the instructions of the other. This experience can be further extended by the children enlarging their maps by increasing the size of the grid squares. This can be easily demonstrated on an overhead projector. Making a map twice as big leads to trebling the size and so on. Work on area and square and triangular numbers could all flow from the initial mapwork.

## Music

Music featured in nautical life. Sailors had their own special dances and songs. Sea shanties were work songs designed to help with the laborious mechanical activities such as winding the capstan. Singing was led by the shanty man who also made up new verses to the familiar songs. Children will enjoy making up their own verses to sea shanties such as 'Blow, boys, blow'.

## Drama

Music and drama could be linked in an improvised drama based on life at sea. The crew could join the ship, the capstan manned, the sails raised and rigging climbed. There would be decks to be scrubbed, sails to be repaired, painting and caulking to be finished. Discipline would be harsh and the food poor, however a busy day might end with a traditional sailor's hornpipe.

## Art

A three-dimensional model of Treasure Island could be made, including as many of the features mentioned as possible – e.g. Spy-Glass Hill, not forgetting a model of the ship and the stockade.

A 'Wanted Pirates' frieze could be contributed to by all the children which would include a written description as well as portraits of each pirate. The treasure cave would also make a good subject for individual paintings or group collage work.

# Further Reading

## Non-fiction

**Book about Pirates** (Ladybird: General Interest Series)

**Pirates and Bucaneers** (Piccolo)

**Maps and Symbols** (Blackwells Learning Library)
*J. C. Gagg*

**Sailing Ships for Discovery and Trade** (Macmillan Education)
*R. H. Fice and Iris Simkins*

**Sea Songs and Shanties** (Macmillan Education)
*R. H. Fice and Iris Simkins*

## Fiction

**Treasure Island** (Puffin)
*R. L. Stevenson*

**They Raced for Treasure**
*Ian Serraillier*

**The Cay** (Puffin)
*Theodore Taylor*

**Robinson Crusoe** (Penguin: Listening and Reading)
*Daniel Defoe*

# The Treasure Seekers
*E. Nesbit*

This is the story of a closely-knit family group who become
involved in a series of adventures through attempts to repair
their family fortunes.

## Topic: The family

Children are always interested in things to do with themselves.
Family groups could be looked at – how many children, brothers
and sisters – the role of the mother – does it differ from
father's role – other relations – the idea of the family tree.
Each child could write his own autobiography, beginning with
his earliest recollections through to the present. Other members
of the family, such as pets, could be included.

## Language

Throughout the book, the children are hoping to find treasure.
A major piece of writing could be developed around this theme.
For example, the teacher could prepare a mystery map of a
treasure island with hazards marked which the child will have
to overcome in his imagination and writing, such as – your
ship sinks in shark bay – attacked and captured by cannibals –
scale the ice mountain – spend the night in tiger jungle. This
sort of approach, modified to suit the teacher's own children,
will provide support for less able children and stimulus for the
more able. The latter may well write an extended story over a
number of days. Some children, once they have grasped the
idea, might prefer to invent their own hazards.

The investigation of the family can be extended by writing word
pictures of the members of the family. Attention should be
paid to adjectives used in descriptions, and the portraits could
include character sketches and anecdotal material.

Noises in the night, with their attendant emotions of fear and
apprehension, can stimulate good imaginative writing. What
causes the noises – ghosts, burglars? What do you do? How do
you feel?

## Drama

Movements such as creeping, freezing, spinning around,
shrinking away and finding your way in the dark will form the
basis of a movement session leading into improvisation on the
theme of burglary. For example – the burglars creep towards a
dark house, a twig cracks – they freeze – it's nothing, they

move on. An upstairs window is open, the drainpipe is climbed. They enter the room, someone strikes a match – but it goes out – they search in darkness – suddenly the door is thrown open and the light is switched on!

## Mathematics

As a link with the language work, the children could make their own treasure island maps. Simple grids would help locate features in the map, e.g. in which grid square is the treasure? More able children may be introduced to the notion of scale.

There is much reference to money in the story. Children will sympathize with H.O.'s desire for sweets. Pocket money could be discussed and the idea of saving investigated. Sometimes it is possible to involve children in a class saving activity, e.g. a school fund or a fund for class pets. A bank or post office with a savings department can be set up and cardboard money used for activities.

## Art

A family portrait gallery could be made.

The burglary would make a good subject for large-scale treatment, especially so if painted in sequences as with a comic strip.

A treasure chest might be made out of cardboard boxes with iron bands added in foil paper and treasure (made from clay, milk bottle tops, etc.) stored inside.

A treasure table could be set up on which could be displayed the children's own 'special treasures' with descriptive labels added.

## Further Reading

### Non-fiction

**Me and My Family** (Puffin)
*Mick Wilson*

**Treasure** (Nelson: Lively Readers)
*Leonard Sealey*

### Fiction

**The Barrow Lane Gang** (BBC Publications: Jackanory)
*Noel Streatfield*

**The Family from One End Street** (Puffin)
and
**Further Adventures of the Family from One End Street** (Puffin)
*Eve Garnett*
The everyday adventures of Mr Ruggles, a dustman, Mrs Ruggles, a washerwoman, and their large lively family.

**The Story of the Treasure Seekers** (Puffin)
*E. Nesbit*

# The Wind in the Willows

*Kenneth Grahame*

To many people this remains the greatest children's classic written, but at the same time it is not an easy book for children to read. The characters are familiar to children through the Walt Disney film and the play, Toad of Toad Hall, which is constantly being revived and used in parts or as a whole in schools, and they are characters which become more beloved through familiarity. The Take Part book provides a way into actually reading about Toad and the rest. This is the highest for reading age levels of the series.

## Topic: Environmental studies

The book opens in spring. What sort of sounds would be heard by the river bank in spring? Which flowers would you expect to find? What life would there be in the river? Comparison could be made between life by the river in spring, summer, autumn and winter. A growing familiarity with such seasonal changes could lead to greater enjoyment for both the urban and the rural child when they come to read the descriptive passages in Grahame's original.

Alternatively, the natural element in the story could be approached through the animals themselves. Toad is boastful and conceited. Have you ever seen a frog or toad puffing in and out, like someone puffed up with pride? Why do toads do this? What sort of animals are they? Would a toad like living in a house?

Amphibians like the toad, frog and newt are relatively easy to study in the classroom as spawn or tadpoles, and fully grown specimens are easily available from pet shops or dealers.

The characteristics of the toad can be compared with the three mammals. Mole is an insectivore, rat a rodent and badger a carnivore. Even quite young children enjoy the simple classification of animals.

Toad's delight, first in his caravan, then in his motor car, could lead to a study of the caravan. Who has traditionally used caravans? What are the differences between travelling by car and caravan? The car might be considered as a source of pollution through both noise and fumes and compared on these grounds with a caravan.

## Language

The character in the story who most fascinates children is Toad. The children could be asked to imagine they were Toad and write his story, e.g. 'My New Car', 'How I Tricked Old Ratty', 'In Prison, How I Escaped'. They might tell the story of another Toad craze, e.g., 'What sort of thing would appeal to Toad – perhaps to be an astronaut or to fly an aeroplane?'

The story can be looked at from a different angle. Imagine you are a weasel from the Wild Wood. Tell the story of how you take over Toad Hall. What do you think of it and Toad? Describe the feast and the sudden intrusion.

Toad has certain bad habits which he finds very difficult to give up. Discussion of habits could lead to the children writing about their own bad habits and possible cures.

At the end of the story Toad sings a final song. Individually or in groups the children could make up another Toad song or poem about events in the story or to celebrate a new adventure.

## Drama

Improvisations based on events from the story, such as the banquet, or an event which is referred to, e.g. the Trial of Toad, would involve large groups.

Early in the story Ratty and Mole have a picnic. This could be taken as a theme for a drama lesson. For example – everyone is asleep – the cock crows. All awake, clothes are donned, faces washed and the picnic is packed. By car, foot and rail people travel to their picnic destinations in the country, by the river, at the seaside. After the day's events, which may be as exciting and dramatic as the teacher and children wish to make them, the children return home and go to bed, thus ending the lesson on a quiet, relaxed note.

## Art

Models of cars and caravans could be made in a variety of materials.

A river scene provides scope for collage work, special attention being paid to the season.

A dramatic frieze of the banquet scene showing the moment of entry of Toad and his friends could be made. The characters in the painting could be shown with speech balloons coming out of their mouths. If the teacher does the final lettering for the frieze, then all the class can participate in the reading of these balloons.

## Music

Percussion work could concentrate on the liquid sounds of the river in spring and summer. Drums and blocks can be used to evoke the caravan with the clip clop of the horse or the speed of the motor car and cymbals employed for the crash.

Toad's song can be chanted or sung to a percussive accompaniment, and of course songs from the stage play can be learnt.

# Further Reading

## Non-fiction

**Amphibians and Reptiles** (Macdonald: Junior Reference Library)

**Badgers** (Wheaton: Read About It)
*Eileen Everett*

**Life in Fresh Water** (Macdonald: Junior Reference Library)

**Moles** (Wheaton: Read About It)

**Nature Awake and Asleep** (A. & C. Black)
*Elsie Proctor*

**Rivers and River Life** (Macdonald: First Library)

**Toads** (Wheaton: Read About It)
*Eileen Everett*

## Fiction

**Tarka the Otter** (Puffin)
*Henry Williamson*
Tells the story of the life and death of a Devon otter. It is written with extreme understanding and sensitivity, and the life of a wild creature is imaginatively portrayed. The otter's patience and tenacity are detailed with enormous admiration and knowledge.

**The Owl Hoots Twice at Catfish Bend** (Puffin)
*Ben Lucien Burman*
The animals at Catfish Bend were living contentedly together under their leader, wise old Doc Raccoon, until a sly grey fox from the City asked for hospitality.

**The Wind in the Willows** (Methuen)
*Kenneth Grahame*

**Watership Down** (Puffin)
*Richard Adams*

# The Wizard of Oz

## L. F. Baum

This story is the one of the group which contains most 'magic', but at the same time it keeps its feet firmly rooted in the practicalities of life with a very business-like heroine and a series of characters all with a purpose in finding the Wizard. Moving as it does from a natural disaster into a world of mystery and magic, the story provides opportunities for both factual and imaginative work.

## Topic 1: Natural phenomena

Why do thunderstorms, cyclones, hurricanes, earthquakes, tidal waves and volcanic eruptions occur? What is the result of such natural disasters? (Newspapers could be referred to for reports of such events.)

Some disasters have become part of history and myth. The story of Noah's flood is one of the earliest recorded disasters. Children will be interested in the story of Pompeii. Consideration could be given to the geographical location of disasters. Immigrant children may well be able to recount experiences of such occurrences.

The cyclone cellar underneath the farm house can be compared with the bomb shelters of the Second World War. Children might find out about these shelters from their parents or grandparents.

In some parts of the world, special materials are used for building in order to combat the effects of disasters, e.g. the Japanese paper house.

## Topic 2: Magic

Magic and superstition is a theme which is of perennial interest to children of all ages.

The history of witchcraft and the superstitions surrounding it can be explored where appropriate. This exploration could include good and bad magic, witches, warlocks, wizards, spells, the apparatus, e.g. cauldron, broomstick and cat. The children will be interested in talking about their own superstitions, e.g. jumping over cracks in the pavement, crossing their fingers and so on.

The ideas of lucky numbers and colours, birth signs and birth stones, horoscopes and the place of the stars can all be explored. For a more detailed analysis of this subject see Lane and Kemp's *An Approach to Topic Work in the Primary School*.

# Language

All children have experienced extremes of weather in our climate. They could be asked to describe their feelings in a thunderstorm. What noises do they hear, what do they see? A dramatic element could be added – imagine you are in a forest when a thunderstorm starts. Metaphors based on the weather could be discussed and lists of expressions compiled, such as 'I was thunderstruck' and 'he came into the room like a hurricane'.

As a component on their work on magic, spells might be devised, bearing in mind such things as – 'Is your spell to have a good or bad effect?' 'Who is it aimed at?' 'What special words will you use?' 'If there is a potion or brew, what are the ingredients and how should they be mixed?' The spells might be made into a class book, suitably decorated, including spells for regaining courage, hearts and brains. As part of the preparation for this work selected extracts can be read from *Catweazle* and the witches' scenes in *Macbeth*.

The characters who accompany Dorothy all lack some fundamental human element. The Tin Woodman has no heart. What effect would this have? The children could be asked to think about the feelings they have and to describe those things they are most fond of. Many children will sympathize with the Lion's lack of courage and be able to write about their own fears and how they overcome them. The characters' problems are solved by their helping one another. The importance of friends could be discussed.

## Drama

Improvisations on themes connected with magic usually produce lively results. The cauldron will serve as a focal point for activities. Chants and incantations based on those in *Macbeth* will strengthen confidence in the oral aspects of drama.

## Further Reading

### Non-fiction

**Lucky Charms** (Blackie: Our Wonderful World)
*Sheila M. Lane and Marion Kemp*

**Tricks and Magic** (Ladybird)

# Fiction

**A Wizard of Earthsea** (Puffin)
*Ursula Le Guin*
A tale of wizards, dragons and terrifying shadows in which the young wizard Sparrowhawk strives to destroy the evil shadow-beast he has let loose in the world.

**Catweazle** (Puffin)
and
**Catweazle and the Magic Zodiac** (Puffin)
*Richard Carpenter*
For once, one of Catweazle's magic spells really does work, and he flies from his eleventh-century cave to the twentieth century, with all its mysterious and magic inventions. Serialized on TV.

**Glinda of Oz** (Collins: Young Armada)
*L. Frank Baum*

**The Marvellous Land of Oz** (Collins: Young Armada)
*L. Frank Baum*

**The Wizard of Oz** (Dent)
*L. Frank Baum*

**Wizards are a Nuisance** (BBC Publications: Jackanory)
*Norman Hunter*

# The Wombles

*Elisabeth Beresford*

The fact that these stories are so familiar to children makes this an ideal choice for young readers. One of the Wombles' most endearing traits is that they make the most of the things that they find.

## Topic: Waste

A project on waste could start with children re-reading the text and listing finds mentioned in the story. What other things do human beings throw away? Think for instance about kitchen waste. In the story Wombles are waste removers – how is our domestic waste removed? What happens to it? Waste can be classified into two basic sets – 'useless' and 'recyclable'. Children can be taken on a Womble Hunt in the local environment and the waste they find can be sorted, labelled, investigated and exhibited. The idea of pollution will arise naturally from such work and the effects of the human life style on the natural world makes a fruitful area of investigation.

Domestic refuse has long been a source of information to archeologists, e.g. clay pipes, Roman pottery. Children might end their project by making a 'time capsule' of twentieth-century waste for future generations to puzzle over. They may also like to form their own Womble club and help to keep Britain tidy.

## Language

On pages 35–38 the Wombles discuss the, to them, unfamiliar game of golf. Children could be asked to write a factual account of the game they play. The test of course is what happens when somebody tries to play following their written instructions. This idea could be extended to include other everyday activities such as making a cup of tea.

The Wombles are great collectors and the children can be encouraged to go 'wombling' for words. Womble sacks could be displayed around the classroom with each sack labelled appropriately. For example labels might include phonic families, compound words (see Chapter 7), homonyms (see page 28) etc. The children could contribute to these sacks with the teacher writing the words on the front of the sack.

## Art

The Wombles waste nothing and this idea can be utilised in art work. Corks, bottle tops, matchboxes and other items can be used for printing. String, twine and wool make interesting string prints. Tin labels and cuttings from magazines make good materials for collage. A giant figure of a Womble might be made from these. Larger pieces of junk such as egg boxes, cornflake packets etc, are ideal for junk modelling. Children can also do their own recycling by soaking and mashing paper and egg boxes for papier mâché work.

## Music

The familiar Womble song could be sung to a percussion accompaniment. Rather than using bought instruments children could make their own using waste materials. For example, shakers and rattles can be made from containers of any shape or size filled with items such as dried peas, salt, pebbles etc. Any metal implements will ring when hung from a string and struck with a spoon. A slither box can be made from a small box filled with beads or rice. Yoghurt pots can be hit together. Jingles can be made by threading milk bottle tops, buttons or beads onto string. The instruments will appear more attractive if decorated.

## Drama

A Womble dance could be improvised to fit the musical accompaniment suggested above. Womble costumes could be made from newspaper and string. This dance could be used as the centre piece of a Womble Midsummer party – perhaps with a feast, games and entertainment. The whole could then be performed, perhaps at an assembly, where it would serve as the inauguration of a school litter campaign.

## Further Reading

### Non-fiction

**Fun to Make Music** (Hamlyn)
*A. Kemp*

**Archaeology** (New Horizon Library: Sampson Low)

**Pollution** (Macdonald First Library: Macdonald)

**Pollution and Life** (Blandford)
*A. Darlington*

**The Know How Book of Puppets** (Usborne)

**Working with Odds and Ends** Vol 8
(Colourcrafts Macdonald)

**Fun with Paper Modelling** (Kaye and Warde)
*G. C. Payne*

**Keep Britain Tidy Kit**

# Take Part Starter Books

The purpose of Starters is to introduce children to the Take Part series.

Take Part Starters are organized in three levels:

Level 1 consists of stories for two parts
Level 2 consists of stories for three parts
Level 3 consists of stories for four parts

Each book in a level contains four short stories chosen because they will be encouraging and rewarding to children at an early stage in their reading development and to those who are experiencing difficulties in achieving fluency.

The stories are derived from traditional sources and cover a wide interest range.

A child reading a Take Part Starter for the first time should be matched with one who can read at the 8-year-old level with some fluency. In this way there can be a natural exchange of one-to-one dialogue. The part at reading age 6 is written in such a way that the text has a very low readability level. The aim is to make this first experience of Take Part reading pleasurable and successful.

The three and four part stories give experience in following the text and moving in and out of dialogue.

The material is of great value for use during short periods with small groups of children. At the end of each story there are follow-up activities which involve the children in the exploration of the text. These can be either individual or group activities.

The titles in the Take Part Starter Books are:

Level 1 (stories for 2 parts)
  The Clever Little Tailor and other stories
Level 2 (stories for 3 parts)
  The Princess and the Frog and other stories
Level 3 (stories for 4 parts)
  William Tell and other stories

Additional titles are in preparation for each of the three Take Part Starter levels.

# Take Part Books
Reading age levels, authors, ISBNs

## Reading Age Levels

**Beaverbird** *Ruth Underhill*
0 7062 3488 X

Beaverbird 9+    Palil 7
Blackcap 9    Yama 7
Grandfather 8    Edal 6+
Big Shellnose 8    Bone Nose 6+
Woman captive 7    Red Fish 6+
Old Man slave 7

**Brer Rabbit** *Joel Chandler Harris*
0 7062 3494 4

Brer Rabbit 9    Brer Wolf 7+
Brer Terrapin 9    Brer Bear 7+
Brer Fox 9

**Children of the New Forest**
*Captain Marryat*
0 7062 3777 3

Edward Beverley 9    Alice Beverley 7
Jacob Armitage 9    Edith Beverley 6+
Humphrey Armitage 9 Pablo 6+

**Chitty-Chitty-Bang-Bang**
*Ian Fleming*
0 7062 3489 8

Commander Pott 9+    Mimsie Pott 8
Joe the Monster 9    Bob-Bon 8
Man-Mountain Fink 8    Driver 7
Garage Man 7    Jeremy 6+
Soapy Sam 7    Jemima 6+
Blood-Money Banks 7

**The Family from One End Street**
*Eve Garnett*
0 7062 3605 X

Mrs Ruggles 9+    Kate 8
Lily Rose 9    James 7+
Mr Ruggles 8+    John 7

**Flat Stanley** *Jeff Brown*
0 7062 3490 1

Mrs Lambchop 9    College friend 8
Mr Dart 9    Luther 8
Mr Lambchop 8    Stanley 7+
Dr Dan 8    Max 7
Policeman 8    Arthur 6+

**The Land of Oz** *L. Frank Baum*
0 7062 3633 5

Woggle-Bug 9+    Saw-Horse 8
Tip 9+    Tin Woodman 7+
Guard 9    Jack Pumpkinhead 7
King Scarecrow 8+

**The Last of the Mohicans**
*J. Fenimore Cooper*
0 7062 3753 6

Major Duncan    Cora Munro 8
Heyward 9+    Uncas 7+
Hawkeye 9+    Magua 7+
David Gamut 9    Alice Munro 6+
Old Delaware Chief 8+

**The Merry Adventures of
Robin Hood** *Howard Pyle*
0 7062 3487 1

Robin Hood 9
The Lord Bishop of Nottingham 9
King Richard the Lionheart 9
Little John 8
The Sheriff of Nottingham 8
Will Scarlet 7
Midge, the Miller's Son 7
Friar Tuck 7

**Mystery at Black Pony Inn**
*Christine Pullein-Thompson*
0 7062 3650 5

Mr Pemberton 9
Ben 9
Commander
  Cooley 8+

Lisa 8+
Harriet 8
James 7
Paul 7

**Parsley and the Herbs** *Michael Bond*
0 7062 3495 2

| | Parsley's Tail | Parsley's Good Deed | Parsley's Problem Present |
|---|---|---|---|
| Sir Basil | 8 | 8 | – |
| Lady Rosemary | 9 | 9 | – |
| Parsley | 8 | 8 | 9 |
| Bayleaf | 8 | 8 | – |
| Constable Knapweed | 7 | 7 | 7 |
| Sage | 6 | 6 | 7 |
| Dill | 6 | 6 | 8 |
| Mr Onion | – | – | 8 |

**Six Folk Tales** *Leila Berg*
0 7062 3496 0

*The Soup-Stone*
Old Man 7+
Good Woman 6

*Anansi and the Pudding Tree*
Anansi 8
Kisander 7
Mouse 6

*The Billy-Goats Gruff*
Troll 8
Big Billy-Goat Gruff 7+
Little Billy-Goat Gruff 7
Second Billy-Goat Gruff 6+

*The Woman who Always Argued*
Old Man 8
Old Woman 7
Friend 6

*Rabbit and Elephant*
Elephant 8
Rabbit 7+⁻
Farmer 7

*Uncle Bouki and the Horse*
Clever Dick 8
Uncle Bouki 7+
Mean Old Man 7

**Space Hostages** *Nicholas Fisk*
0 7062 3625 4

Flight Lieutenant 9+
Brylo 9+
Tony 9

Sandra 8
Spadger 7+
Di 7
Ashley 7

**Stories from Grimm**
0 7062 3754 4

*Hansel and Gretel*
Wicked Witch 8
Hansel 8
Gretel 6+

*Briar Rose or Princess Rosebud*
Good Fairy 9
King 8+
Queen 7

Princess Rosebud 7
Prince 7+
Bad Fairy 6+

*Rumpelstiltskin*
Miller's Daughter 8+
Messenger 8
Rumpelstiltskin 7
King 6+

**Treasure Island** *Robert Louis Stevenson*
0 7062 3776 5

Doctor Livesey 9+
Jim Hawkins 9
Captain Smolett 8+
Long John Silver 8+
Squire Trelawney 8

Israel Hands 7+
Ben Gunn 7+
Tom Morgan 7
Redruth 6+
George Merry 6+

**The Treasure Seekers** *E. Nesbit*
0 7062 3497 9

Dicky 8
Albert's Uncle 8
A Visitor 8
Albert-next-door 7
Horace Octavius 6+

Dora 9
Oswald 9
Noel 7
Alice 6+

**The Wind in the Willows**
*Kenneth Grahame*
0 7062 3486 3

Rat 9
Toad 9

Badger 8
Mole 7

**The Wizard of Oz** *L. F. Baum*
0 7062 3491 X

Dorothy 9
The Scarecrow 9
The Wicked Witch of the West 8+
Glinda 8
A Munchkin 8
The Wizard of Oz 8
The Lion 7+
The Tin Woodman 7
The Good Witch of the North 7
A Guard 7
A Winged Monkey 6+

**The Wombles** *Elisabeth Beresford*
0 7062 3604 1

Tomsk 7
Orinoco 8
Great Uncle Bulgaria 7+
Bungo 9
Tobermory 9+

# Take Part Starter Books

Level 1 (stories for 2 parts)
**The Clever Little Tailor** and other stories
reading levels between 6 and 8

Level 2 (stories for 3 parts)
**The Princess and the Frog** and other stories
reading levels between 6 and 8

Level 3 (stories for 4 parts)
**William Tell** and other stories
reading levels between 6 and 8